A Snowman's Path

Peggy Soucek

Halo
PUBLISHING
INTERNATIONAL

A Snowman's Path
Copyright © 2021 Peggy Soucek
Illustrated by Peggy Soucek
Scripture is taken from King James Version
All rights reserved.

No part of this book may be reproduced in any manner whatsoever without the prior written permission of the publisher, except in the case of brief quotations embodied in reviews.

ISBN: 978-1-61244-974-6
LCCN: 2021902848

Halo Publishing International, LLC
8000 W Interstate 10, Suite 600
San Antonio, Texas 78230
www.halopublishing.com

Printed and bound in the United States of America

I dedicate this book to my first granddaughter Allison and to her loving parents, my daughter Rose and her husband Nick, who started reading to her as an infant.

I love you,

Mom/Grandma Peggy

Some days the wind is fun.

James 1:6

For he who doubts is like a wave of the sea driven and tossed by the wind.

Some days the sun is brighter.

Psalm 113:3

From the rising of the sun to the place where it sets, the name of the Lord is to be praised.

Some days I eat snacks.

Psalm 111:5

He provides food for those who fear Him;

He remembers His covenant forever.

Some days we visit others.

Psalm 133:1

How wonderful and pleasant it is when brothers live together in harmony.

Some days I might forget to floss.

Amos 4:6

Also I gave you cleanness of teeth in all your cities.

Psalm 81:10

Open your mouth wide and I will fill it

Some days I think I look funny.

Psalm 139:14

I am fearfully and wonderfully made.

Genesis 1:27

So God created man in His own image, in the image of God He created him; male and female He created them.

Some days I learn God's laws.

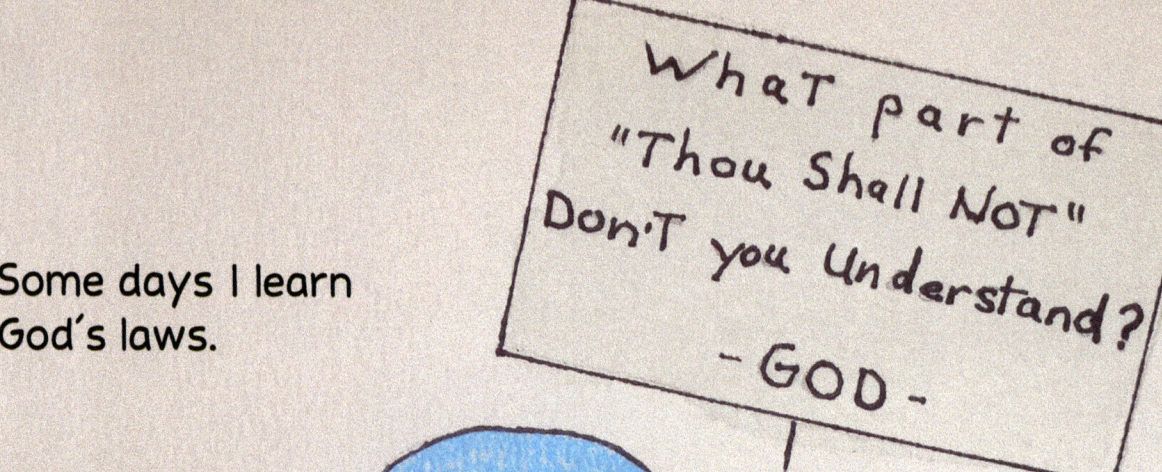

Deut 5:17 to 21

You shall not murder. You shall not commit adultery. You shall not steal. You shall not bear false witness against thy neighbor. You shall not covet your neighbor's wife or anything that is your neighbor's.

Acts 5:29

We ought to obey God rather than men.

Some days I just need to stay calm.

Ephesians 4:2

Be completely humble and gentle; be patient, bearing with one another in love.

Some days I can hear God's voice.

"MY SHEEP HEAR MY VOICE"

John 10:27

My sheep hear my voice, and I know them, and they follow Me.

Some nights I need more sleep.

Psalm 121:4

He who watches over Israel will neither slumber nor sleep.

1 Cor 15:51

We shall not all sleep, but we shall all be changed, in a twinkling of an eye, at the last trumpet.

Some days I feel so free. Like a kite.

John 8:36

If the Son sets you free, you will be free indeed.

Some days I feel light as a balloon.

Isaiah 55:9

For as the heavens are higher than the earth, so are My ways higher than your ways...

Psalm 25:1

To You, oh Lord I lift up my soul.

Some days I want a cooler.

Proverbs 20:1

Wine is a mocker,
strong drink is a brawler...

Ephesians 5:18

Do not get drunk with wine, drinking too much alcohol can lead to disgrace.

Some days I want a treat.

Proverbs 23:18

For surely there is a hereafter.

Gen 1:1

In the beginning God created the heavens and the earth.

Some days my flowers wilt.

Song of Solomon 2: 11 to 12

Behold, the winter is passed; the rain is gone.

The flowers appear on earth the time of singing has come.

Some days I think I am good at sports.

Isaiah 40:31

Those who hope in the Lord will renew their strength. They will soar on wings like eagles, run and not grow weary; they will walk and not be faint.

Some days I sing and play songs.

Psalm 96:1

Oh sing to the Lord a new song; sing to the Lord, all the earth.

Psalm 150:4

Praise Him with stringed instruments...

Some days I go fishing.

Matthew 4:19

Follow Me, and I will make you fishers of men.

Every morning I rise.

Isaiah 33:10

"Now I will rise," says the Lord.

1 Thess 4:17

We who are alive and remain shall be caught up together with them in the clouds, to meet the Lord in the air and always be with the Lord.

Some days I just want to bless you.

Jeremiah 31:3

Yes I have loved you with an everlasting love; therefore with loving kindness I have drawn you.

Someday I'd like to swing on a star.

Could be swingin' on a star

you

Rev 22:16

I am the root and the offspring of David, the bright and morning star.

Sometimes, if I get lonely, I know there is a friend nearby.

ICED MOCHA LATTE

Matthew 6:26

Look at the birds of the air; they do not sow or reap or stow away in barns, yet your heavenly Father feeds them.

Are you not much more valuable than they?

God Bless you!
Peggy Soucek :)

CPSIA information can be obtained
at www.ICGtesting.com
Printed in the USA
BVHW022015160221
600242BV00004B/108